# THE
# PARTHENON

## Peter Chrisp

WAYLAND

# GREAT BUILDINGS

THE COLOSSEUM

THE EMPIRE STATE BUILDING

THE GREAT PYRAMID

THE HOUSES OF PARLIAMENT

THE PARTHENON

THE TAJ MAHAL

Produced for Wayland (Publishers) Limited by
The Creative Publishing Company
Unit 3, 37 Watling Street, Leintwardine
Shropshire SY7 OLW, England

Series designers: Ian Winton and Sally Boothroyd
Book designer: Sally Boothroyd
Editor: Sabrina Crewe
Illustrations: Mike White and Clive Spong
Map: Peter Bull

First published in 1997 by
Wayland (Publishers) Limited
61 Western Road, Hove
East Sussex BN3 1JD, England

**British Library Cataloguing in Publication Data**
Chrisp, Peter
The Parthenon : how it was built and how it was used. -
(Great Buildings)
1.Parthenon (Athens, Greece) - Juvenile literature
2.Temples - Greece - Athens - Juvenile literature
I.Title
726.1'208'09385

ISBN 0 7502 1993 9

Printed and bound in Italy by G. Canale & C.S.p.A., Turin

# CONTENTS

▲ Animal sacrifice was important to the ancient Greeks. They believed the smoke from the roasting meat carried their offerings up to the gods. This carving from the Parthenon shows sacrificial animals on their way to the altar on Athene's birthday.

# ATHENE'S BIRTHDAY PARTY

It was the birthday of the goddess Athene, protector of the city of Athens. Thousands of Athenians made their way in a procession to the Acropolis, or 'high city'. This rocky hill was a holy place where the most important temples stood. Towering over the Acropolis itself was a marble temple to Athene called the Parthenon.

In the centre of the procession was a cart, shaped like a boat with a tall mast, from which a bright yellow piece of cloth hung like a sail. The cloth was a new robe, woven for the ancient wooden statue of Athene which was housed on the Acropolis. It was her birthday present.

The Athenians climbed the hill, leading a hundred oxen and sheep, which were also gifts for Athene. They were led to the altar, a high platform near the Parthenon. One by one, the animals' throats were cut. Some of the meat was burned at the altar; the rest was roasted over open fires for the people. This was a treat, for they rarely ate meat. As they sat enjoying their picnic, they looked up at their beautiful temple, the Parthenon, its milky-white marble shining in the sun.

# CHAPTER ONE

# ATHENS AND ANCIENT GREECE

▼ As part of their system of democracy, the Athenians held open-air meetings on a hill called the Pnyx, west of the Acropolis. Here all the citizens could speak in debates and decide laws by voting.

The ancient Greeks never belonged to a single nation. For over 650 years, from about 1,000BC, every Greek lived in a polis, one of the hundreds of city states on the Greek mainland or on the islands and coasts of the Mediterranean Sea. The Greeks said that their city states were scattered about the Mediterranean like frogs sitting around a pond. The tiniest was the island of Delos, with just five square kilometres of land. Athens ruled over the land of Attica, which at 2,600 square kilometres was one of the biggest.

◀ Each city state had its protector amongst the gods. This relief was carved on the occasion of an Athenian decree honouring the city state of Samos. It shows Hera, protector of Samos, on the left, with the goddess Athene of Athens.

Each city state had its own government and laws. Athens invented a system called democracy, meaning 'people power'. Every citizen of Athens had a say in how the city state was governed. They also served as judges, lawyers and juries in trials. In wartime, they became soldiers.

Only men born of Athenian parents were citizens. Women were not citizens and neither were men who had settled in Athens from other Greek cities. There were also thousands of slaves – men and women who had no rights at all. They had been captured in wars, bought from foreign slave traders, or brought up in Athens as the children of slave parents. Of the 300,000 people who lived in Attica, only one in six was an Athenian citizen.

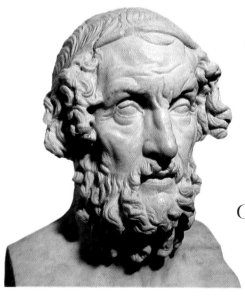

Greece is a land of long dry summers and mild winters. The fine weather allowed Greek men to spend much of their time outside, with their fellow men. The heart of Athens was the agora, or market-place, where the men met each day to argue about politics and law cases, or just to chat.

Greek men were very competitive. Rival city states were always quarrelling and going to war with each other. Within each city, the men all tried to outdo each other. Athenian playwrights and poets competed for prizes.

▲ A Roman bust of the Greek poet Homer, who is thought to have written two famous long poems, The Iliad and The Odyssey, more than 2,500 years ago. These poems were recited from memory in competitions at religious festivals. Homer was so important to the ancient Greeks that he was known simply as 'the Poet'.

▶ This carving shows a woman preparing grain for making bread in ancient Greece, in the 5th century BC.

Artists and architects tried to make more beautiful works than their rivals. Every speaker in the public meetings wanted to make the best speech. Everything was seen as a competition.

While Greek men spent most of their days outside, women mostly stayed indoors. They spun wool and wove it into clothes. They looked after children and gave orders to the household slaves. Their one public role was to serve goddesses, like Athene, as priestesses.

### Games and sport

This detail from a jar, called an amphora, shows a chariot race. Sport was very important to the ancient Greeks. The festivals in honour of the gods usually included contests, such as running and chariot races. The Greeks loved watching these races, and believed that their gods enjoyed them too. The most famous games of all were held at Olympia in honour of Zeus, ruler all of gods. These multi-sport games are still held today – the Olympic Games have become a worldwide event, held every four years.

'Women are better than men. They care for the home and look after goods brought over the sea. Without a wife, no home is clean and prosperous. As to religion, we women play the most important role…. Women conduct rites for the goddesses which would be unholy for men to perform.'

A female character from a play by Athenian playwright Euripedes

▼ This detail from a cup illustrates the Greek myth of Athene's birth. Hephaestus, god of fire and metalworkers, has just split open the head of Zeus, seen here holding his thunderbolts. According to legend, Athene sprang from Zeus' head, fully grown and armed with a shield.

The Athenians worshipped many different gods whose temples could be found all over Attica. The temple of Poseidon, god of the sea, for example, stood at Cape Sounion, overlooking the waves. The goddess of wheat, Demeter, was worshipped at Eleusis, sixteen kilometres west of Athens.

To the Athenians, the most important of all the gods was Athene, goddess of wisdom, war and crafts. She was believed to have shown the Athenians how to grow their most important crop, the olive tree. She invented the potter's wheel and taught women how to weave. She gave her name to the city, which belonged to her.

There was an old story about how the land had come to belong to Athene. People said that there had once been a contest between Athene and Poseidon. The two gods met on the Acropolis where each claimed the right to rule Attica. The local people had to choose between the two gods. Poseidon struck the Acropolis rock a great blow with his trident. Immediately, sea water began to flow from the hole. This meant that Poseidon was offering the city power over the sea. Then Athene lightly touched the rock with her pole and the very first olive tree sprouted. This was her gift to the city, and it won the contest.

The Athenians knew exactly where the two gods had stood when they met on the Acropolis. There was still a mark in the rock left by Poseidon's trident. Athene's sacred olive tree still grew there.

▼ Athene is seen as the goddess of war in this bronze statue. In her warrior form, she was known as Athene Promachus ('she who fights in the front ranks').

### Greek mythology

The ancient Greeks believed their many gods were part of a large family. The gods of Greek mythology had many human characteristics, but they were immortal and immensely powerful. Zeus was the most powerful god, as he ruled the sky and Earth. His brothers had their own kingdoms also: Poseidon ruled the sea and Hades the underworld, or kingdom of the dead. All the gods had areas, such as music, fire and hunting, that they represented or taught to humans. The Greeks had many myths about the antics of their gods, who fought and competed amongst themselves as well as looking after humans.

11

# CHAPTER TWO

# THE GREEKS AND THE PERSIANS

▼ A Greek soldier, called a hoplite (or foot soldier) is shown in this picture from a vase, painted around 480BC. Scenes of war, like many other aspects of life in ancient Greece, were used to decorate jars and dishes of all kinds.

Between 558 and 500BC, the Persians – the people of the country that is now Iran – conquered the biggest empire the world had known. It stretched from Egypt to the borders of India and had taken over the eastern Greek cities. Forty million people lived under Persian rule.

Unlike Athenian citizens, who governed themselves, everybody in the Persian Empire had to obey the will of the king. The Athenians thought that this was as bad as being a slave. So when the eastern Greeks rose up against the Persians, in 499BC, the Athenians sent a fleet of warships to help them. Despite this help, the Greek uprising was crushed.

The Persian king, Darius, now wanted to punish Athens. In 490BC, he sent an invasion force of 600 ships to the plain of Marathon, north east of Athens. The Athenian army rushed to Marathon where, greatly outnumbered, they decided

'The Athenians were triumphant, chasing the enemy, and cutting them down until they reached the sea, and men were calling for fire and taking hold of the ships.'

Herodotus the historian, describing the battle at Marathon.

to attack. Gripping their shields, they charged down the hillside towards the Persians. It was an amazing victory for the Athenians: some 6,400 Persians were killed, but the Athenians lost only 192 men.

The Athenians were certain that their success was due to the help of their goddess, Athene. To celebrate and thank her, they decided to build a big new temple on the Acropolis. It was called the temple of Athene Parthenos ('the virgin'), or the Parthenon.

▲ The court of Darius the Great is shown on this relief. Standing behind the throne is Xerxes, the son of Darius who succeeded him as king.

◄ Greek warriors do battle with Persians on this monument from Asia Minor. The Greeks called all foreigners 'barbarians', people whose speech sounded meaningless, like the sounds 'bar-bar-bar'. The Persians were considered the worst barbarians of all.

The defeat at Marathon was a terrible disaster for the Persians. When the news reached their empire, there were more uprisings against Persian rule. These kept the Persians busy for almost ten years. However, in 480BC, the Persians invaded Greece again, this time to conquer the whole country. Their new king, Xerxes, son of Darius, led an army which was so big that it seemed unbeatable.

As the Persians marched towards Athens, the Athenians, with no chance against the huge army, abandoned their city. They crossed in ships to the neighbouring island of Salamis, taking with them their most prized possession, the wooden statue of Athene. Finding Athens deserted, the Persians set fire to it. They destroyed the temples on the Acropolis, including the half-built Parthenon. From Salamis, the Athenians would have seen their city go up in flames.

Xerxes now sent his huge fleet against the Athenians at Salamis. The Greek ships were outnumbered, but they were faster and they had bronze battering rams. They darted between the

◀ A warship shown in a mosaic from ancient Greece. At the prow is the battering ram with which enemy ships were attacked.

slow Persian ships, snapping their oars and ramming them. Xerxes watched in horror as his fleet was destroyed.

The Athenians returned to their city and began to rebuild their homes. But they did not repair the temples – the ruins were left as a reminder of the terrible behaviour of the Persians. There was one piece of good news: Athene's sacred olive tree had not been killed by the fire. From its blackened branches, it put out new green leaves, a sign that the goddess was still watching over Athens.

▼ This lion devouring a calf is thought to be a carving from the pediment of the original Parthenon, which was ruined by the Persians when they invaded the deserted city of Athens.

After Salamis, it was the turn of the Greeks to go on to the attack. In 478BC, they held a great meeting on the tiny island of Delos. It was attended by Greeks from hundreds of city states, mostly from the eastern islands. They agreed to join together in a league to attack Persia.

Each member of the League of Delos promised to give something to build up a great war fleet. The Athenians had already shown their skill at winning sea battles, and they had the biggest fleet. Many city states found it simpler to give money rather than build their own ships. As a result, Athens supplied the ships, the soldiers, and the generals who commanded the fleet.

When two islands tried to leave the league, the Athenians sent their fleet to punish them. Athens was growing more and more powerful. At first, the league's money was kept on Delos, but in 454BC the Athenians took the treasure to Athens. They said that this was for safekeeping, but it meant that the Athenians could now do whatever they liked with the money.

▼ The market-place at Delos, where the great meeting of Greek city states took place. Delos was believed to be the birthplace of the god Apollo. This made it one of the holiest places in the world to the Greeks. It was so important that the much bigger neighbouring islands were called the Cyclades, meaning those 'around' Delos.

Most of the money was used to pay for the war against Persia. However, the Athenians kept some for their goddess, Athene. This meant that the members of the league were now paying tribute, or tax, to Athens. Little by little, the league had turned into the empire of Athens.

▼ A map of the Athenian Empire around 450 BC.

BLACK SEA

ADRIATIC SEA

0    50    100   150   200km
0         50        100 miles

Byzantium

Bisanthe

Amphipolis

THASOS

SAMOTHRAKE

IMBROS

LEMNOS

AEGEAN SEA

LESBOS

EUBOIA

Eretria

KHIOS

Kolophon

ATTICA

Salamis

SAMOS

IONIAN SEA

Athens

KEOS

ANDROS

TENOS

AIGINE

Olympia

DELOS

PAROS

NAXOS

KOS

Sparta

MELOS

RHODES

MEDITERRANEAN  SEA

KARPATHOS

The Athenian Empire

CRETE

# CHAPTER THREE

# THE PLAN FOR THE PARTHENON

▼ The city states controlled by Athens were forced to stop using their own coins. They had to use Athenian coins, each one showing Athene and her sacred bird, the owl.

By about 450BC, the Persians were no longer a threat to Greece. The Athenian warfleet had freed the cities of the eastern Greeks from Persian rule. These cities were forced to join the Athenian Empire, which was now at its most powerful.

Pericles, who was leader of the Athenians, wanted Athens to look like a city which ruled a great empire. Around 450BC, he suggested using the money collected from the allies to rebuild the temples which had been burned by the Persians. This money had been given for the war against Persia, and some citizens said it was wrong to use it for any other purpose. Pericles replied: 'It is only fair that after

Athens has been equipped with all she needs to carry on the war, she should use the rest for public works, which, once completed, will bring her glory for all time.'

Pericles won the argument. The first temple to be planned was a new Parthenon for Athene. It was to be built on the base of the half-finished temple destroyed by the Persians.

The Parthenon was to be the work of the whole city. Hundreds of ordinary citizens, foreign workers and slaves helped in the actual building work. All the citizens had a role of some kind in the building of the temple. Every decision was discussed in the public meetings, and every single payment had to be approved by the citizens of Athens.

**Pericles (499 – 429 BC)**
Pericles was the man who had led the Athenians to power. He was the most influential of Athenians; almost every year, from 461BC to his death in 429BC, he was re-elected as general. He was a clever man who knew how to win over the citizens at their public meetings. A poet called Eupolis later remembered Pericles with these words: 'He was the greatest speaker of all...he cast a spell on us.' According to the Greek historian Plutarch, Pericles had a very long forehead, which is why he is always shown wearing a helmet.

Here you can see the little temple of Athene Nike (meaning 'of victory') on the right, with its Ionic columns. Towards the middle are the Doric columns of the Propylaea, the huge gateway to the Acropolis.

The Greeks had fixed ideas about what a temple was supposed to look like, for they had been building them for hundreds of years. Their earliest temples were made of wood and mud-brick. When the Greeks began to build in stone, around 700BC, they copied many of the features of wooden buildings. Even wooden pegs, used to fix larger parts together, were copied in stone.

There were two styles of temple building, which developed in different parts of the Greek world. The Greeks on the mainland invented a simple, sturdy style called Doric. The eastern Greeks invented a more

**Optical illusion**
Although the Parthenon seems perfectly rectangular (top), it was designed with subtle curves (bottom) that enhance its strength. The bulge of the columns makes them seem more imposing. They also tilt inwards as they rise, which exaggerates their height. The columns at the edges are slightly thicker and more closely spaced than the rest – this makes the corners, which stand out against the sky, look stronger.

decorative style called Ionic. The easiest way to tell them apart is by looking at the capitals, the tops of the columns. The Ionic capital is decorated with two swirls.

The Athenians used both Doric and Ionic styles of architecture. When they wanted to build a big, imposing structure, they chose the strong Doric style. For smaller temples, they preferred the lighter Ionic style. Both styles are used on the Acropolis.

The Parthenon was designed by two architects, called Ictinus and Callicrates. Their aim was not to design a new type of building, but to make the most perfect Doric temple possible. They had a strict set of rules to follow about proportions and shapes. They knew what a Doric temple had to look like.

Doric capital

Ionic capital

# BUILDING THE PARTHENON

W ork on the Parthenon began in 447BC. It was one of the few Greek buildings to be made completely out of marble. The 22,000 tonnes of marble used to build the Parthenon came from a quarry on Mount Pentelicus, sixteen kilometres away. The blocks were cut by hand and lowered down the mountainside. They were then taken to Athens on carts pulled by teams of oxen.

At the Acropolis, the stone carvers shaped the marble into drum-shaped blocks, for the columns, and rectangular blocks, for the walls. Every block had to be perfect, because no mortar was used to join them. The wall blocks were fixed with iron clamps, wrapped in lead to stop them rusting. The drums were joined by a pin set in a hole in the centre. Ten or twelve drums were used in each column.

Only the tops and bottoms of the drums were finished before assembly. Once they had been heaved into place, they were cut back to their final surface. The aim was to make each column look like a single piece of marble.

▼ Every block and column drum of the Parthenon had to be precisely measured and designed. The individual curves or angles of each piece fitted together to form the final impression of straight lines and immense strength.

**Building the Parthenon**
1. Wall block
2. Scaffolding
3. Lifting tongs
4. Column drum
5. Hoist
6. Oxen bringing stone

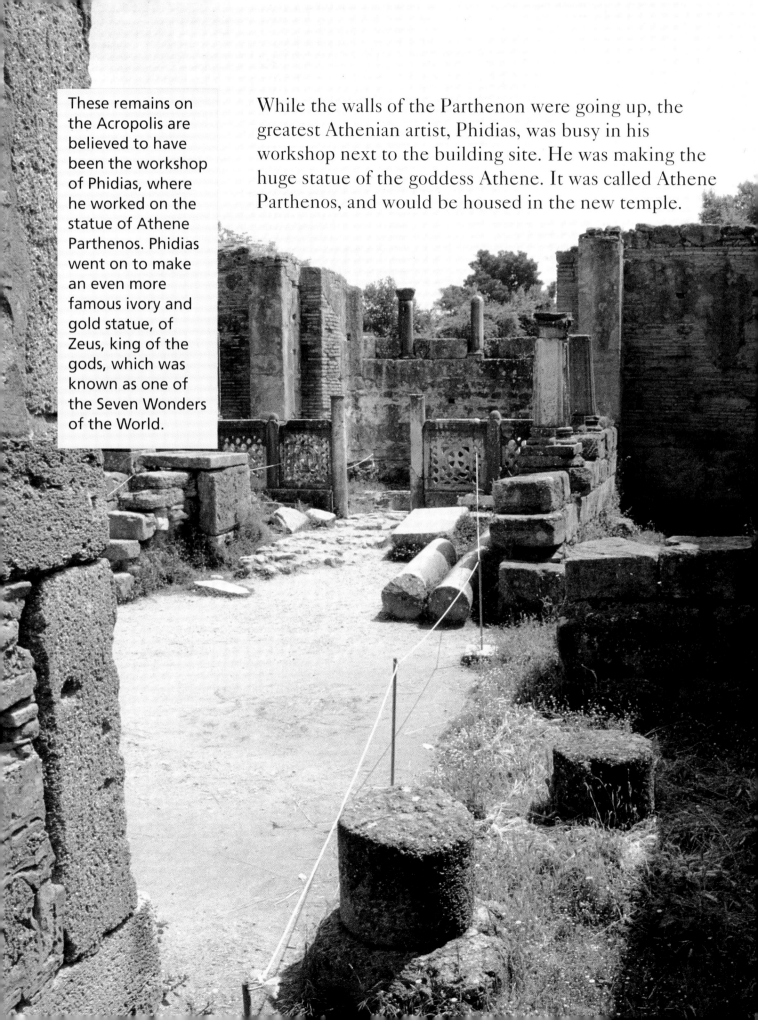

These remains on the Acropolis are believed to have been the workshop of Phidias, where he worked on the statue of Athene Parthenos. Phidias went on to make an even more famous ivory and gold statue, of Zeus, king of the gods, which was known as one of the Seven Wonders of the World.

While the walls of the Parthenon were going up, the greatest Athenian artist, Phidias, was busy in his workshop next to the building site. He was making the huge statue of the goddess Athene. It was called Athene Parthenos, and would be housed in the new temple.

The statue, which was over twelve metres high, was made of wood covered with precious materials. The goddess' skin was ivory, using elephant tusks brought by sea from Egypt. Her clothing and armour were made of 100 kg of gold. These materials meant that the statue of Athene cost more to make than the whole Parthenon. A great deal of work went into the statue. Athene's face, more than two metres high, was made out of hundreds of tiny ivory strips. More detail went into her gold shield and sandals, which were covered with pictures of legendary battle scenes.

The statue was placed in the middle of the temple, facing the east door and the rising sun. There was a shallow pool of water just in front of the goddess. This was partly to stop the ivory cracking in the dry air. But it also reflected the light up on to Athene's face. At sunrise, with her golden dress and white face gleaming with reflected light, the statue must have looked overwhelming.

'The hands of Phidias alone were able to give birth to gods.... Those were the good old days for Greece!... When she had an artist unmatched by any that later ages produced; when it was possible to show men how the gods looked.'

The Greek writer Philo of Byzantium, in about 225 BC

▼ Although the Parthenos no longer exists, it was so famous that many smaller versions were made over the centuries. This one in the Museum of Athens is called the Varvakeion. In one hand, she holds a statue of the winged goddess of victory – this figure was as large as a human being on Phidias' original Parthenos.

As well as making the giant statue of Athene, Phidias was in charge of the design of the sculptures which decorated the outside walls of the Parthenon. He had a large team of skilled sculptors to do the actual carving.

There were three types of sculpture on the Parthenon. The first pieces to be carved were the metopes, square blocks carved with scenes of single combat. They showed gods fighting giants, and Greeks grappling with centaurs (who were half-horse and half-man) or Amazon warrior women. The sculptors then carved a frieze, which went all the way around the wall of the temple. The last job was to carve enormous statues for the pediments. Each end showed an event in the story of Athene: the east pediment showed her birth, while the western end depicted her contest with Poseidon.

▼ In this nineteenth-century painting by Sir Lawrence Alma-Tadema, Phidias is standing on scaffolding next to the Parthenon frieze, showing it to the admiring Athenians. You can see the brightly painted band of figures along the building, making their great procession.

## The mystery of the Parthenon frieze

The figures of the frieze are taking part in a religious procession to celebrate Athene's birthday. But why are there no hoplites, who would almost certainly have been part of the procession? Why does the frieze show 192 horses and riders that wouldn't have actually been there? Some people believe they represent the 192 soldiers lost at the battle of Marathon. The Greeks believed the souls of dead heroes sometimes rode up to meet the gods on Mount Olympus. There are many theories about what the frieze represents, but the mystery remains.

pediment

frieze

metope

The sculptors began by sketching an outline on a slab. Then they cut away, using hammer and punch, and then chisels of various sizes. The surface was sanded and polished, and shining bronze fittings, such as weapons and bridles, were added. The figures were then painted, like all Greek sculpture. Women were shown as pale-skinned, while the men were tanned. This indicated their different ways of life.

CHAPTER FIVE

# WORSHIP ON THE ACROPOLIS

The Acropolis was a holy place. It was the highest point of the city, where the earth met the heavens, the home of the gods. It had been the religious centre of Athens for hundreds of years before the Parthenon was built.

## Inside the Parthenon

This nineteenth-century engraving shows what the interior of the Parthenon would have looked like when it was completed. The Parthenon was the treasury of the Athenian empire. Tribute, war trophies and offerings to the goddess were all kept in the storeroom behind the statue. The statue itself was seen as a store of gold. The golden armour and clothing were made of plates which could be removed in time of need. The Athenians believed that Athene would be happy to give up the gold if her city needed it.

After the Parthenon was finished in 432BC, other new buildings went up on the Acropolis. These included the Erectheion, which housed the ancient wooden statue of Athene; the little temple to Athene Nike; and a big building, the Propylaea, which acted as the gateway to the Acropolis.

You can still see these buildings if you visit Athens today. Many other features of the ancient Acropolis have disappeared. It was covered with war trophies – armour and weapons captured in war hung everywhere as reminders of Athens' success in war. There was a big bronze statue of Athene Promachos in her armour, also made by Phidias.

'And so the buildings rose up, as imposing in their sheer size as they were graceful, since the artists strove to excel themselves in the beauty of their workmanship. Yet the most wonderful thing about them was the speed with which they were finished. They were created in such a short space of time, to last for all time.'

The Greek writer Plutarch, in the second century AD.

29

## The Erectheion

The Erectheion was the holiest place on the Acropolis, home to the ancient olive wood statue of Athene and a shrine to several gods and early kings. It has a small porch with columns carved in the shape of women, known as the Caryatids. The other porch contains the rock which the ancient Greeks believed was struck by Poseidon in his contest with Athene. Her own sacred olive tree grew just outside.

Temples such as the Parthenon were not places for group worship – they were the homes of the gods whose statues they contained. The actual religious ceremonies, like much of Greek life, took place in the open air.

Throughout the year, the Athenians had many religious festivals. The processions and sacrifices celebrated different gods and involved different rituals. The festival of Artemis, goddess of wild animals, was celebrated with a dance performed by little girls pretending to be bears. During the Panathenaia, Athene's birthday festival, little boys danced holding shields.

The Panathenaia was the biggest and most important festival in Athens. It began with contests: running and chariot races, and musical and poetry competitions. Prizes were jars of olive oil, each decorated with a painting of Athene. After the contests was the great procession, when the goddess' new dress was wheeled up to the Acropolis, followed by the animal sacrifices on the great altar.

### Athene's servant girls

Every year, two little girls, aged between seven and eleven, were chosen to live on the Acropolis. They were called the Arrephoroi, and they were there to keep Athene company and act as her special servants. After a year they went back to their families and two new girls were sent in their place. It was a great honour to be chosen, but the Acropolis must have been a lonely place at night, when everyone had gone home.

▲ The priestess of Athene on the right is about to set out two cushioned seats, which her attendants are carrying. This is part of the Parthenon frieze, which depicts the Panathenaic procession on Athene's birthday.

The Greek city states lost their freedom in 338BC, when they were conquered by King Philip of Macedon. Then, in 146BC, the Romans arrived. Greece became part of the enormous Roman Empire.

The Parthenon stood unchanged. Phidias' famous statue was visited and admired by Roman tourists. The Athenians still celebrated their goddess' birthday, wheeling their wooden ship up the winding hill of the Acropolis. All this had to stop when Christianity became the official religion of the Roman Empire, in the fourth century AD. The old gods, including Athene, were now said to be devils. Sacrifice was banned. The statues of the old gods were destroyed.

The Christians had an effective way of winning people over. They would take a Greek temple and turn it into a church, dedicated to a saint who was most like the god who had been worshipped there. Around AD450, the Parthenon became a church, dedicated at first to 'Holy Wisdom' and then to the Virgin Mary, mother of Christ. So people now went to the Parthenon to pray to the Virgin of Athens rather than to Athene the Virgin.

To turn the temple into a church, changes had to be made. Unlike a temple, a church was a place for group worship. The religious ceremonies took place inside the building rather than outside by an altar. So the two rooms were knocked into one, to hold the worshippers. At the eastern end, an apse was added, a curved extension to house the Christian altar. The inside was richly decorated with religious paintings. The ceiling was given a great mosaic, a picture made up of tiny tiles, showing the Virgin Mary.

▲ This nineteenth-century engraving shows the Roman army as they invaded and conquered the Greeks in 146BC.

▶ A fourteenth-century Greek mosaic of the Virgin Mary, who had taken over from Athene as the Virgin of Athens. The Parthenon was a Christian church for a thousand years, 150 years longer than it had been Athene's temple.

In the Middle Ages, Athens passed from one foreign ruler to another. The city was captured by the French (1205); then the Catalans from Spain (1311); and then the Florentines of Italy (1385). These invading peoples were all Christian, and the Parthenon continued to serve as their church.

Everything changed when the Turks arrived, capturing Athens in 1458 after a two-year siege. The Turks converted the Parthenon into a mosque, a Muslim place for prayer. They whitewashed over the Christian wall

▶ The Turks were Muslims, followers of the religion of Islam. From the 1320s, they had been fighting a holy war against the Christians of Greece. Under their greatest leader, Sultan Mehmed the Conqueror (right), they swept across the Greek territories, conquering the city of Constantinople in 1453 and Athens in 1458.

paintings, for Muslims did not approve of art showing human figures. In spite of this they left the original Greek sculptures undamaged, perhaps because they were so difficult to reach. On the outside of the building, the Turks added a minaret, a tall tower from which the faithful were called to prayer. The voice of a muezzin sang out five times a day from the minaret: 'Come to prayer! Come to security! God is most great!' The Turks further altered the appearance of the Acropolis by building several small houses around the temples.

By the 1600s, Athens had shrunk into a small and unimportant town. It was now that the first wealthy European travellers began to arrive, as tourists. They had read about the Parthenon in books by ancient Greek and Roman writers. They wanted to see if the temple lived up to its descriptions, and they were not disappointed. Most of the sculptures were well preserved. The milky-white marble still sparkled.

▲ This drawing from the sixteenth century shows how the Parthenon looked during the 200 years it served as a mosque. You can see the minaret that was built on to the roof by the Turks.

'The most beautiful piece of antiquity remaining in the world.'

George Wheler, a British visitor to the Parthenon in 1682.

# CHAPTER SIX

# THE PARTHENON BESIEGED

▼ In the explosion of 1687 the roof of the the Parthenon, most of its inner walls, and the tops of the middle columns at the side were all destroyed. A fire burned on the Acropolis for two days before it could be put out.

In September 1687, the city of Athens was besieged yet again. The attacking army came from Venice in Italy. The Venetians hoped to drive the Turks out of Greece and conquer the country for themselves.

Outnumbered, the Turkish defenders moved up on to the Acropolis. They hoped that the Venetians would not

VEDUTA DEL CAST: D'ACROPOLIS DALLA PARTE DI TRAMONTANA.

fire directly at the temple with its famous sculptures. So they stored their gunpowder inside, and the women and children sheltered there.

General Francesco Morosini cared only about taking the city. He found out where the gunpowder was stored, and ordered his men to fire their cannon at the Parthenon. On the evening of 26 September, the whole city was shaken by a deafening explosion. It killed 300 people, and the Turks surrendered. The Parthenon, which had survived for over 2,000 years, was in ruins.

**Venetian vandalism**
The Venetians held on to Athens for less than seven months before they abandoned the city. Morosini did further damage to the Parthenon when he tried to remove the central statues on the western end to take back as souvenirs to Venice. His clumsy workers dropped them, smashing them to bits.

▼ The Turks returned to Athens after the Venetians left, and found the Parthenon in ruins. It could no longer be used as a mosque. The Turks took stones from the temple to build a little mosque inside its walls, which you can see in this nineteenth-century painting.

▼ The Elgin Room at the British Museum in 1819. Lord Elgin had brought back half of the frieze showing the religious procession, fifteen of the metopes showing single combat, and twenty of the big statues of gods from the pediments.

Foreign visitors still went to admire what was left of the Parthenon. Some found bits of sculpture lying on the ground and took them away as souvenirs. The greatest souvenir hunter of all was the wealthy Earl of Elgin, who was fascinated by ancient Greek art and architecture.

In 1799, when he was ambassador to Turkey, Elgin discovered that the Turks were not looking after the Parthenon and its sculptures. He obtained permission to remove 'pieces of stone with old inscriptions and figures' from the Acropolis. This may have meant only that Elgin could take stones which were lying around on the ground. But Elgin used the permission to start sawing off carvings still on the temple. These sculptures were shipped to Britain, and went on show in London in 1807.

In 1816, Lord Elgin sold the Parthenon carvings to the government, and they were moved to the British Museum. Everyone rushed to see the 'Elgin Marbles', as they were now called. They were the best examples of Greek art that anyone had seen. A painter, Henry Fuseli, shouted excitedly, 'By God! The Greeks were gods!'

### Greek art hits the West
When the Elgin Marbles arrived in Britain, there was already a growing taste for Greek art. People admired it because of its 'ideal beauty'. The Greeks only showed the human body at its most perfect. Every country wanted to get its hands on ancient Greek art. The keenest collectors were the Germans, the French and the British. In the early 1800s, more Greek temples were stripped of their statues, which ended up in museums in Paris, Munich, Berlin and London.

▲ In the nineteenth century, Greek architecture had a huge influence across the western world. Grand public buildings, such as libraries, law courts and museums, were modelled on Greek temples like the Parthenon. The British Museum itself, where the Elgin Marbles are housed, is such a building.

# CHAPTER SEVEN

# RESTORING THE PARTHENON

▶ The Battle of Navarino took place on 20 October 1827. The aim of the allies (Britain, France and Russia) was to put pressure on the Turks to make peace. In the battle, 53 Turkish ships were sunk without a single allied loss.

In 1837, the Greeks formed an Archaeological Society to look after the ancient buildings. Anything on the Acropolis which was not ancient was pulled down. The little temple of Athene Nike was rebuilt, and some of the fallen columns of the Parthenon were repaired. Meanwhile, at the foot of the Acropolis, a modern city began to grow.

In the 1820s, when the Parthenon sculptures were causing a sensation in western Europe, dramatic events were taking place in Greece. After 400 years of Turkish rule, the Greeks were fighting for their freedom.

It was a long and bloody war. To stop the fighting and help the Greeks, the governments of Britain, France and Russia sent a combined fleet of 27 warships to southern Greece. At the Battle of Navarino in 1827, they destroyed the entire Turkish warfleet. By 1830, the Greeks were a free people.

The ancient ruins of the Acropolis were important to the new Greek nation, as a reminder of their glorious past. It was because of this that Athens, a little town of 300 houses, was chosen to be the new capital.

'These stones are more precious than rubies.... It is to these stones that we owe our rebirth as a nation.'

Iakovos Neroulos, President of the Greek Archaeological Society, speaking in 1837 at the ruins of the Parthenon.

▼ These sculptures from the Parthenon pediment are displayed at the British Museum. The damaged figures include the goddesses Demeter and Persephone, originally part of an enormous scene depicting Athene's birth from the head of Zeus.

In the early 1800s, an Englishman called John Cam Hobhouse was travelling in western Greece, at that time still ruled by the Turks. He met an old Greek man who said to him: 'You English are carrying off the works of the Greeks, our forefathers. Look after them well. Greeks will come and ask for them back.'

Ever since Greece became a free nation in 1830, the Greeks have asked for the Parthenon sculptures to be returned to Athens. From time to time, British people have also called for their return. However, the British Museum has refused to give the marbles back. Like many European museums, the British Museum is filled with foreign works of art. If it returned one object to its country of origin, it might have to return them all.

Today Athens, like most modern cities, has a bad problem with pollution. In the hot summer, the fumes from cars and chimneys make a dense smog which hangs over the city. This eats away at the marble on the Acropolis. In winter, acid rain attacks the stones. As long as this problem remains, the statues cannot be put back on the walls of the Parthenon. However, the Greeks hope that one day they will get back the sculptures and display them in a museum by the Acropolis, placing copies on the temple itself.

'The Parthenon marbles are to the Greek nation a thousand times more dear and more important than they can ever be to the English nation, which simply bought them.'

Frederic Harrison, 1890, in a newspaper article entitled 'Give Back the Elgin Marbles'

▲ The Parthenon is still under restoration. The skin of the marble, which has been eroded by traffic fumes and acid rain, is being patched. Metal rods, used to repair the columns 150 years ago, have rusted and are being replaced. Those rods which survived the 1687 explosion, made by the ancient Greeks 2,500 years ago, have lasted much better.

# TIMELINE

## 700-501BC

**c700** First stone temples built by the Greeks

## 500-451BC

**490** Persians invade Greece and are defeated at Marathon by the Athenians

**498-80** Athenians begin building the first Parthenon

**480** Persians invade Greece again, sacking Athens and burning the temples on the Acropolis. The Athenian fleet defeats the Persians at Salamis

**478** League of Delos formed by Athens and other states to fight Persia

**460** Phidias builds a 27m high bronze statue of Athene to stand on the Acropolis in the open air

## 450-401BC

**447** Building of a new Parthenon begins on the base of the old one

**438** Phidias' gold and ivory statue of Athene set up inside the Parthenon, which is complete apart from the statues in the pediments

**438-432** Carving of the statues of the gods for the pediments

**430-404** War between Athens and Sparta, ending with the defeat of Athens

## 400BC-AD199

**338** King Philip of Macedon conquers Greece

**146BC** Greece becomes part of the Roman Empire

## AD200-1299

**390** Christianity becomes the only religion allowed in the Roman Empire

**c450** Parthenon converted into a Christian church

**1205** Athens captured by the Franks, or French

## AD1300-1599

**1311** Franks driven out by the Catalans, from southern Spain

**1385** Catalans driven out by the Florentines, from Italy

**1456-8** Turks capture Athens and lay siege to the Acropolis, which eventually surrenders

**c1460** Parthenon converted into a Muslim mosque

## AD1600-1799

**1687** Athens besieged by the Venetians. They fire cannon at the Parthenon, where the Turks are keeping their gunpowder, and cause a terrible explosion

**1688** Turks return to Athens

## AD1800-2000

**1801** Lord Elgin begins to remove carvings from the Parthenon

**1821-30** Greeks fight against the Turks for their freedom

**1834** Athens becomes capital of the kingdom of Greece

**1836-42** Temple of Athene Nike rebuilt

**1984** Work begins on the restoration of the Parthenon

# GLOSSARY

**Acropolis**
High city. Most Greek cities had an acropolis, a place to take refuge if the city was attacked, and also the site of the city's main temples.

**Altar**
A flat-topped block or platform, usually outside a temple, where offerings to a god were made.

**Antiquity**
Something belonging to ancient times.

**Citizens**
People who have full rights as members of a particular state. In ancient Greece, only men could be citizens.

**Decree**
An order made by a person in a position of power, or by an authority such as a government or council.

**Festival**
A celebration. Greek festivals were always in honour of their gods. They were marked by sports, drama, music and animal sacrifice.

**Frieze**
A continuous band of pictures.

**Ivory**
The hard, tooth-like substance from which animal tusks are formed. Elephant ivory is still used to make decorative objects, although in many parts of the world killing elephants for their ivory is against the law.

**Muezzin**
The man who calls Muslims to prayer.

**Relief**
An image which is carved or moulded to stand out from its background.

**Rites**
A sequence of actions and words which is always done in the same way on a particular occasion, such as a religious sacrifice or baptism.

**Sacrifice**
The killing of an animal as an offering to a god.

**Trident**
A spear with three points.

# FURTHER INFORMATION

## BOOKS

David J. Brown, *How They Were Built*, Kingfisher, 1991

John Ellis Jones, *Ancient Greece*, History as Evidence series, Kingfisher, 1992

Joanne Jessop, David Salariya, *The X-Ray Picture Book of Big Buildings of the Ancient World*, Watts, 1992

Fiona MacDonald, *A Greek Temple*, Inside Story series, Simon and Schuster Young Books, 1992

Anne Pearson, *Ancient Greece*, Eyewitness series, Dorling Kindersley, 1992

Richard Wood, *Architecture*, Legacies series, Wayland, 1994

## CD-ROMS

*History of the World*, Eyewitness series, Dorling Kindersley Multimedia, 1995

Picture acknowledgements

The publishers would like to thank the following for allowing their pictures to be reproduced: Lesley and Roy Adkins: pages 24, 43; Ancient Art & Architecture Collection: pages 4, 6, 8 (bottom), 11, 13 (top and bottom), 14 (top), 16-17, 25, 29; Bridgeman Art Library: pages 26 (Birmingham City Museums and Art Gallery), 37 (The Fine Art Society), 42 (British Museum); British Museum: pages 35, 38; C M Dixon Photo Resources: pages 7, 14-15, 18, 22; Mary Evans Picture Library: pages 32, 40; Werner Forman Archive: pages 33, 34 ; Michael Holford Photographs: pages 8 (top), 9, 10, 19, 20-21, 27, 31; Tony Stone Images: front cover (Vic Thomasson), pages 30, 39, 40-41; Wayland Picture Library: pages 3, 12, 44, 45.

# INDEX